WILLIAMS-SONOMA

FOODMADEFAST
one pot

RECIPES
Carrolyn Carreño

GENERAL EDITOR
Chuck Williams

PHOTOGRAPHY
Tucker + Hossler

Oxmoor
House®

contents

about this book

When you make supper using the carefully crafted recipes in this book and just one or two pots, you'll spend less time on preparation and cleanup and still prepare delicious, healthy meals with little effort. Easy techniques, such as braising and roasting that maximize the flavor of a few well-chosen ingredients are the key to preparing dishes that taste rich and flavorful, as though you have been in the kitchen for hours.

Simple dishes like Apricot-Glazed Chicken and Barbecue Beef Sandwiches are ideal for serving on hectic weeknights. Recipes such as savory Pork Chops with Cider Glaze and Spanish Paella are special enough for festive occasions. Whether you are whipping up a weeknight supper for your family or you are entertaining guests, you'll find that the delicious recipes and labor-saving tips in Food Made Fast *One Pot* will help you to put a healthy, home-cooked meal on the table every night of the week.

Chuck

30 minutes
start to finish

herbed sweet potatoes with feta

Sweet potatoes, 4 large, peeled and cut into slices ½ inch (12 mm) thick

Olive oil, 3 tablespoons

Salt and freshly ground pepper

Feta cheese, ¼ lb (125 g), crumbled

Pine nuts, ⅓ cup (2 oz/ 60 g)

Fresh thyme, 1 tablespoon finely chopped

Juice from 1 lemon

SERVES 4–6

1 **Season the sweet potatoes**
Preheat the oven to 400°F (200°C). Place the potatoes in a 2-qt (2-l) gratin or baking dish. Drizzle with the oil, season with salt and pepper, and toss to coat. Spread the potatoes in a single layer.

2 **Bake the sweet potatoes**
Cover the dish with aluminum foil and bake for about 20 minutes. Uncover, sprinkle evenly with the feta, pine nuts, and thyme, and continue to bake, uncovered, until the cheese is golden and the sweet potatoes are tender, 8–10 minutes longer. Remove from the oven, drizzle evenly with the lemon juice, and serve.

cook's tip

Serve this classic German-inspired dish with the traditional accompaniment of whole-grain mustard and pumpernickel or toasted rye bread.

baked sausages with herbed beans

1 Cook the sausages and onions

Preheat the oven to 400°F (200°C). In a large Dutch oven over medium-high heat, warm 1 tablespoon of the oil. Add the sausages and cook, turning occasionally, until browned on all sides, about 5 minutes. Transfer to a plate. Add the remaining 1 tablespoon oil and the onion and sauté until softened, 3–4 minutes. Add the garlic and thyme and cook until fragrant, about 1 minute. Pour in the chicken broth and bring to a simmer.

2 Cook the beans

Add the beans with their liquid and the tomato pureé to the pot and cook until the liquid begins to thicken, about 2 minutes. Season with salt and pepper. Return the sausages to the pot.

3 Bake the dish

In a small bowl, stir together the bread crumbs, Parmesan, and 1 teaspoon oil. Sprinkle the bread crumb mixture over the top and bake until golden brown, about 20 minutes. Let cool slightly before serving.

Olive oil, 2 tablespoons, plus 1 teaspoon

Hot or sweet Italian sausages, 4 large, about 1 lb (500 g) total weight

Yellow onions, 2 large, halved and thinly sliced

Garlic, 2 cloves, minced

Thyme, 2 tablespoons, chopped

Chicken broth, 1 cup (8 fl oz/250 ml)

Cannellini beans, 2 cans (15 oz/470 g each)

Tomato pureé, 1/4 cup (2 oz/60 g)

Salt and freshly ground pepper

Fresh bread crumbs, 1/4 cup (1/2 oz/15 g)

Parmesan cheese, 1/4 cup (1 oz/30 g) freshly grated

SERVES 4

spinach & cheese
stuffed chicken

Olive oil

Baby spinach, 2 cups
(2 oz/60 g), chopped

Fresh goat cheese, ¼ lb
(125 g), crumbled

Parmesan cheese, ½ cup
(2 oz/60 g) freshly grated

**Salt and freshly ground
pepper**

**Skinless, boneless chicken
breast halves,** 4, about
1½ lb (750 g) total weight

Prosciutto or cooked ham,
4 large thin slices

SERVES 4

1 Prepare the filling
Preheat the oven to 400ºF (200ºC). Oil a shallow
baking dish just large enough to hold the chicken breasts
in a single layer. In a small bowl, mix together the spinach,
goat cheese, and Parmesan. Season with salt and pepper.

2 Stuff the chicken
Place each chicken breast on a work surface. Holding
a sharp knife parallel to the work surface, cut each breast in half
lengthwise almost all the way through. Spread one-fourth
of the spinach-cheese filling in the center of each breast. Fold
the chicken breast closed and season with salt and pepper.
Wrap 1 prosciutto slice tightly around each chicken breast and
place in the prepared dish.

3 Bake the chicken
Bake until the prosciutto is crisp and the chicken
is opaque throughout, about 20 minutes. Divide among
individual plates and serve.

cook's tip

A variety of ingredients can
be used to stuff chicken
breasts. In place of the spinach
and Parmesan, use roasted
red peppers (capsicums) and
feta cheese. Add some lemon
zest for a spark of citrus.

cook's tip

To add extra flavor to the stew, you can make cheese or herb dumplings. Simply stir 1 cup (4 oz/125 g) grated Cheddar or asiago

cheese or 1 tablespoon finely chopped fresh chives, basil, or parsley into the dry ingredients in Step 2 and proceed with the recipe.

chicken stew with dumplings

1 Cook the chicken and vegetables

Season the chicken with salt and pepper. In a Dutch oven over medium-high heat, melt the 2 tablespoons butter. Add the chicken and cook, stirring often, until golden, about 4 minutes. Add the carrots, onion, and celery, season with salt and pepper, and cook until the vegetables begin to soften and the chicken is opaque, 4–5 minutes. Sprinkle with the 2 tablespoons flour and cook, stirring, for about 2 minutes. Gradually pour in the chicken broth, add the peas, and bring to a boil.

2 Make the dumpling dough

Meanwhile, in a medium bowl, combine the 2 cups flour, the baking powder, and 1 teaspoon salt. Using a pastry blender or 2 knives, cut in the ½ cup butter until the mixture forms coarse crumbs the size of peas. Add the milk and stir, then knead a few times until the mixture forms a soft dough.

3 Finish the stew

Drop heaping tablespoons of the dough over the top of the boiling stew. Reduce the heat to low, cover the pot, and cook until the dumplings have nearly doubled in size, 7–10 minutes. Sprinkle with the parsley and serve.

Skinless, boneless chicken thighs, 1½ lb (750 g), cut into bite-sized pieces

Salt and freshly ground pepper

Unsalted butter, ½ cup (4 oz/125 g), cut into small pieces, plus 2 tablespoons

Carrots, 3, thinly sliced

Yellow onion, 1, chopped

Celery, 2 stalks, thinly sliced

Flour, 2 cups (10 oz/315 g), plus 2 tablespoons

Chicken broth, 4 cups (32 fl oz/1 l)

Baby peas, ½ cup (2½ oz/75 g)

Baking powder, 2 teaspoons

Milk, ½ cup (4 fl oz/125 ml)

Fresh flat-leaf (Italian) parsley, 2 tablespoons minced

SERVES 4

pork chops with cider glaze

Bone-in, center-cut pork loin chops, 4, each about ¾ inch (2 cm) thick

Salt and freshly ground pepper

Olive oil, 2 tablespoons

Red cabbage, 1 head, halved, cored, and thinly sliced crosswise

Apple cider or apple juice, 2½ cups (20 fl oz/625 ml)

Apple cider vinegar, 1 tablespoon

Fresh thyme leaves, 1 tablespoon

SERVES 4

1 **Brown the pork chops**
Season the pork chops generously with salt and pepper. In a large frying pan over medium-high heat, warm the oil. Add the pork chops and cook, turning once, until golden, about 5 minutes total. Transfer to a plate. Add the cabbage to the pan and cook, stirring, until softened, 3–4 minutes.

2 **Make the glaze**
Raise the heat to high, pour the cider and vinegar over the cabbage, and boil until the liquid is reduced to about 1 cup (8 fl oz/250 ml), 8–10 minutes. Stir in the thyme.

3 **Finish the pork**
Return the pork chops and any accumulated juices to the pan and spoon the glaze over them. Cover, reduce the heat to medium-low, and simmer until the pork is tender and barely pink inside, about 5 minutes. Arrange the cabbage and pork on a platter, top with the glaze, and serve.

cook's tip

If you have the time, brine the pork chops overnight. It is an easy process that makes for exceptionally flavorful meat. In a large bowl, combine 4 cups (32 fl oz/1 l) apple cider, 3 cups (24 fl oz/750 ml) water, ½ cup (4 oz/125 g) salt, 5 peppercorns, and 2 cinnamon sticks. Immerse the chops in the liquid, cover, and refrigerate for at least 6 hours or up to overnight.

cook's tip

When fresh basil is in season, use it to garnish the halibut. To cut the basil leaves into strips, stack the leaves on top of one another and roll them tightly lengthwise. Use a large chef's knife or kitchen shears to cut the leaves into thin strips.

halibut with tomatoes & leeks

1 Roast the leeks

Preheat the oven to 450°F (230°C). In a large roasting pan, toss the leeks with 2 tablespoons of the olive oil, and season with salt and pepper. Spread the leeks in a single layer. Roast until just tender, about 10 minutes. Remove the pan from the oven and add the tomatoes. Preheat the broiler (grill).

2 Cook the halibut

Season the halibut with salt and pepper, and lay the fillets over the leeks and tomatoes. Drizzle with the remaining 1 tablespoon oil. Broil just until the fillets are barely opaque throughout, about 8 minutes. Divide the fillets among individual plates, top with the leeks and tomatoes, and serve.

Leeks, 3 lb (1.5 kg), white and pale green parts, halved, rinsed, and thinly sliced

Olive oil, 3 tablespoons

Salt and freshly ground pepper

Cherry tomatoes, 2 cups (12 oz/375 g)

Halibut fillets, 4, about 6 oz (185 g) each

SERVES 4

apricot-glazed chicken

Skin on, bone-in chicken breast halves, 4, about 3 lb (1.5 kg) total weight

Salt and freshly ground pepper

Canola oil, 2 tablespoons

Apricot jam, ½ cup (5 oz/ 155 g)

Red wine vinegar, 2 tablespoons

Whole-grain or Dijon mustard, 2 tablespoons

Garlic, 2 cloves, minced

Fennel, 1 large bulb, trimmed, quartered lengthwise, and thinly sliced

SERVES 4

1 **Brown the chicken**
Preheat the oven to 425°F (220°C). Season the chicken generously with salt and pepper. In a large ovenproof frying pan over high heat, warm the oil. Add the chicken and cook, turning once or twice, until golden brown, 8–10 minutes.

2 **Make the glaze and bake the chicken**
Meanwhile, in a bowl, stir together the jam, vinegar, mustard, garlic, and ½ teaspoon salt. Brush the glaze over the chicken breasts, leaving about 1 tablespoon in the bowl. Add the fennel and toss with the remaining glaze. Spoon the fennel over the chicken. Bake until the chicken is opaque throughout, about 10 minutes. Divide among individual plates, spoon the fennel over the chicken, and serve.

cook's tip

Traditional gumbo recipes often
contain shellfish such as crab,
shrimp, or crawfish. If you like,
add ½ lb (250 g) cooked, peeled,
and deveined shrimp (prawns)
when you return the browned
chicken and sausage to the pan.

chicken & sausage gumbo

1 Brown the chicken and sausage

Season the chicken with salt and pepper. In a large saucepan over medium-high heat, melt 2 tablespoons of the butter. Add the chicken and sauté until browned, 2–3 minutes. Add the sausage and sauté until browned, about 2 minutes longer. Transfer the chicken and sausage to a plate.

2 Cook the vegetables

Add the celery, onion, bell pepper and garlic to the pan and cook until the vegetables begin to soften, 3–5 minutes. Add the remaining 2 tablespoons butter and the flour, stirring to incorporate, about 2 minutes. Gradually stir in the broth and bring to a boil.

3 Finish the gumbo

Return the chicken and sausage and any accumulated juices to the pan. Add the okra, reduce the heat to medium, and simmer until the chicken is opaque throughout and the gumbo has thickened, about 10 minutes. Season with salt and pepper, ladle into bowls, and serve.

Skinless, boneless chicken thighs, 3, about 1 lb (500 g) total weight, cut into bite-sized pieces

Salt and freshly ground pepper

Unsalted butter, 4 tablespoons (2 oz/60 g)

Andouille or other spicy smoked sausage, 1 lb (500 g), thinly sliced

Celery, 4 stalks, chopped

Yellow onion, 1 large, chopped

Green bell pepper (capsicum), 1, seeded and chopped

Garlic, 3 cloves, minced

Flour, 2 tablespoons

Chicken broth, 6 cups (48 fl oz/1.5 l)

Okra, 12 pods, cut into ½-inch (12-mm) pieces, or 2 cups frozen okra

SERVES 4–6

25

creamy mushroom stroganoff

Unsalted butter,
6 tablespoons (3 oz/90 g)

Shallot, 1 large, thinly sliced

Mixed fresh mushrooms,
such as shiitake, oyster, and
cremini, 2 lb (1 kg), thinly
sliced

Flour, 2 tablespoons

Dry white wine, 1 cup
(8 fl oz/250 ml)

**Chicken or vegetable
broth,** 1 cup (8 fl oz/250 ml)

Sour cream, ½ cup (4 fl oz/
125 g)

**Fresh flat-leaf (Italian)
parsley,** 2 tablespoons
minced, plus more for garnish

**Salt and freshly ground
pepper**

**Wide egg noodles or
pappardelle,** 1lb (500 g)

SERVES 4

1 Make the sauce

Bring a large pot of water to a boil. In a large frying pan over medium-high heat, melt the butter. Add the shallot and sauté, until lightly golden, 2–3 minutes. Add the mushrooms and cook, stirring, until they have softened and released most of their liquid, about 5 minutes. Add the flour and stir to incorporate. Stir in the wine and the broth and cook until most of the alcohol has evaporated, about 2 minutes. Remove from the heat, and stir in the sour cream and the 2 tablespoons parsley. Season to taste with salt and pepper.

2 Cook the pasta

Meanwhile, add 2 tablespoons salt and the pasta to the boiling water. Cook, stirring occasionally to prevent sticking, until al dente, according to the package directions. Drain, reserving about ½ cup (4 fl oz/125 ml) of the cooking water. Add the pasta to the sauce and toss to combine. Warm briefly over low heat to blend the flavors. Add as much of the cooking water as needed to loosen the sauce, garnish with the parsley, and serve at once.

cook's tip

To make beef stroganoff, use 1 lb (500 g) cooked leftover steak, such as beef sirloin or tenderloin, cut into 1-inch (2.5-cm) cubes. Add to the sauce along with the broth in Step 1.

cajun
shrimp boil

1 **Simmer the potatoes**
Fill a large pot with water and place over high heat.
Add the Old Bay seasoning, onions, garlic, and lemon halves
and bring to a boil. Add the potatoes, reduce the heat to low,
and simmer until the potatoes are tender, 15–20 minutes.

2 **Cook the shrimp**
Add the corn and sausages to the pot and cook for
5 minutes. Remove from the heat, add the shrimp, cover, and
let stand until opaque, about 4 minutes. Drain in a colander
and return to the pot or a large serving bowl, and serve.

**Old Bay or other crab boil
seasoning,** 6 tablespoons

Yellow onions, 2 large,
quartered

Garlic, 1 head, unpeeled and
halved crosswise

2 lemons, halved

**Small red-skinned
potatoes,** 2 lb (1 kg)

Corn, 4 ears, each cut into
thirds

**Smoked pork or chicken
sausages,** 1 ½ lb (750 g),
cut into slices 1 inch (2.5-cm)
thick

Large shrimp (prawns), 3 lb
(1.5 kg), unpeeled and tails
intact

SERVES 6

29

tortellini & vegetable soup

Olive oil, 2 tablespoons, plus more for drizzling

Carrots, 2, halved lengthwise and thinly sliced

Celery, 2 stalks, thinly sliced

Zucchini (courgettes), 2, halved lengthwise and thinly sliced

Salt and freshly ground pepper

Chicken or vegetable broth, 6 cups (48 fl oz/1.5 l)

Fresh cheese tortellini, 1 lb (500 g)

Plum (Roma) tomatoes, 2, chopped

Fresh flat-leaf (Italian) parsley, ¼ cup (½ oz/15 g) chopped

Parmesan cheese, ¼ cup (1 oz/30 g) freshly grated

SERVES 4

1 Sauté the vegetables
In a large saucepan over medium-high heat, warm the 2 tablespoons oil. Add the carrots, celery, and zucchini and sauté until softened, about 5 minutes. Season with salt and pepper. Stir in the broth and bring to a boil.

2 Cook the tortellini
Add the tortellini and cook for 5 minutes, or according to the package directions. Remove from the heat. Stir in the tomatoes and parsley and season to taste with salt and pepper. Ladle the soup into bowls, drizzle with olive oil, sprinkle with the cheese, and serve.

cook's tip

For a traditional Italian version of this hearty vegetable soup, garnish each serving with a spoonful of store-

bought pesto. The pesto adds herbaceous notes to the simple soup. Round out the meal with a loaf of crusty Italian or whole-grain bread.

cook's tip

A loaf of aromatic toasted garlic
bread is a great accompaniment
to this dish. To make garlic bread,
melt 4 tablespoons (2 oz/60 g)
butter with 1 minced garlic clove.
Cut a baguette in half lengthwise.
Using a pastry brush, brush the
garlic butter on the bread. Toast
the baguette in a preheated
broiler (grill) until golden brown.

spicy
steamed clams

1 Cook the onion and tomatoes

In a stockpot over medium-high heat, melt the butter with the oil. Add the onion and red pepper flakes, season with salt, and sauté until the onion is translucent, about 10 minutes. Add the garlic and sauté until fragrant, about 30 seconds. Add the tomatoes and their juice, and cook, stirring, to blend the flavors, for 2 minutes longer.

2 Steam the clams

Raise the heat to high and stir in the wine. Add the clams, discarding any that do not close to the touch. Cover and cook, shaking the pan occasionally, until the clams open, 4–5 minutes. Discard any empty shells or unopened clams. Divide the clams among serving bowls, top with the broth, sprinkle with the basil, and serve.

Unsalted butter,
4 tablespoons (2 oz/60 g)

Olive oil, ¼ cup (2 fl oz/ 60 ml)

Yellow onion, 1, halved and thinly sliced

Red pepper flakes,
½ teaspoon

Salt

Garlic, 2 cloves minced

Whole plum (Roma) tomatoes, 1 can (16 oz/ 500 g), with juice

Dry white wine, 1 cup (8 fl oz/250 ml)

Small clams such as littleneck or Manila, 2–3 lb (1–1.5 kg), scrubbed

Fresh basil, ½ cup (¾ oz/ 20 g) slivered

SERVES 4

33

chicken & vegetable curry

Thai green curry paste, 2–3 tablespoons

Unsweetened coconut milk, 1 can (14 fl oz/430 ml)

Chicken broth, 1 cup (8 fl oz/250 ml)

Sugar, 2 tablespoons

Canola oil, 2 tablespoons

Skinless, boneless chicken breast halves, 1 lb (500 g), cut into 1-inch (2.5-cm) pieces

Zucchini (courgettes), 2, halved lengthwise and cut into ½-inch (12-mm) pieces

Garlic, 1 clove minced

Baby spinach, 4 cups (4 oz/ 125 g)

Juice from 1 lime

Salt

Steamed jasmine rice, for serving

SERVES 4

1 Make the sauce
In a bowl, stir together the curry paste, coconut milk, chicken broth, and sugar.

2 Cook the chicken and zucchini
In a large frying pan over medium heat, warm the oil. Add the chicken and sauté until golden, 4–5 minutes. Add the zucchini and garlic and sauté until tender-crisp, about 2 minutes longer. Transfer the chicken and vegetables to a plate.

3 Finish the dish
Add the sauce to the pan, bring to a gentle boil over medium heat, and cook until thickened, 3–4 minutes. Return the chicken and vegetables to the pan and simmer until the chicken is opaque throughout, about 2 minutes. Add the spinach and lime juice, season with salt, and toss to combine. Spoon the rice into bowls, top with the curry, and serve.

cook's tip

The curry can be turned into
a hearty soup by adding 3½ cups
(28 fl oz/875 ml) of chicken
broth. Or, make a vegetarian curry
by replacing the chicken with
chunks of tofu or vegetables, such
as thinly sliced sweet potatoes,
bamboo shoots, or snow peas
(mangetouts).

cook's tip

To add a bit of smoky heat, toss
the potatoes with 1–2 teaspoons
Spanish smoked paprika along
with the olive oil in Step 1.

mustard-crusted
salmon & potatoes

1 Roast the potatoes

Preheat the oven to 375°F (190°C). In a large roasting pan, toss the potatoes with the olive oil, and season with salt and pepper. Spread the potatoes evenly in the pan. Roast until the potatoes are golden, about 10 minutes.

2 Season the salmon

Meanwhile, in a small bowl, stir together the Dijon and dry mustards. Coat one side of the salmon fillets with the mustard mixture, then sprinkle evenly with the panko, gently pressing to adhere.

3 Bake the salmon

Arrange the fillets in the pan, breaded side up, next to the potatoes. Bake until the fillets are barely opaque, and the topping is golden brown, and the potatoes are tender, 15–18 minutes. Arrange the salmon fillets alongside the potatoes on a platter, sprinkle with parsley, and serve.

Olive oil, 2 tablespoons

Red-skinned potatoes, 1 lb (500 g), quartered

Salt and freshly ground pepper

Dijon mustard, 1/4 cup (2 oz/60 g)

Dry mustard, 2 tablespoons

Salmon fillets, 4, 1 1/2 lb (750 g) total weight, skin removed

Panko **or fresh bread crumbs,** 4 tablespoons (1 oz/ 15 g)

Fresh flat-leaf (Italian) parsley, 1/4 cup (1/2 oz/15 g) chopped

SERVES 4

broccoli &
pancetta frittata

Unsalted butter,
2 tablespoons

Pancetta or thick-cut bacon, 2 oz (60 g), chopped

Broccoli, 1 head, separated into florets

Eggs, 12

Salt and freshly ground pepper

White Cheddar cheese,
½ cup (2 oz/60 g) grated

SERVES 4

1 **Sauté the pancetta and broccoli**
In a large ovenproof frying pan over medium-high heat, melt the butter. Add the pancetta and sauté until slightly browned, about 5 minutes. Add the broccoli and sauté until tender-crisp, about 4 minutes.

2 **Cook the eggs**
In a bowl, whisk together the eggs, ½ teaspoon salt and ½ teaspoon pepper. Spread the broccoli and pancetta evenly in the pan, then pour in the eggs. Reduce the heat to medium-low and cook, without stirring, until the edges begin to set, about 3 minutes. Using a spatula, carefully lift up the edges and let the uncooked eggs run underneath. Continue to cook, without stirring, until the eggs are almost set on top, 5–8 minutes longer.

3 **Finish the frittata**
Preheat the broiler (grill). Sprinkle the frittata evenly with the cheese. Broil until the top is set and the cheese is melted, about 3 minutes. Cut into wedges and serve.

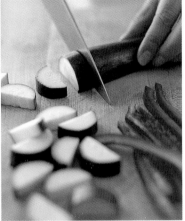

cook's tip

Fritattas often include a variety of chopped vegetables and/or meat and cheeses, which makes them a great way to use leftovers you have on hand.

turkey
poblano chili

1 Brown the vegetables and turkey
In a Dutch oven over medium-high heat, warm the oil. Add the chiles and onion and sauté until softened, about 4 minutes. Add the turkey and cook, stirring to break up any clumps, until the meat begins to brown, 7–8 minutes.

2 Finish the chili
Add the garlic and chili powder, season with salt and pepper and cook, stirring frequently, for 1 minute. Add the tomatoes, beans, and broth. Bring to a simmer, reduce the heat to medium-low, and cook, uncovered, until thickened, about 10 minutes. Season with salt and pepper. Ladle the chili into bowls, garnish with the sour cream, and serve.

Olive oil, 2 tablespoons

Poblano chiles, 2, seeded and chopped

Yellow onion, 1 large, chopped

Ground (minced) turkey, 2 lb (1 kg)

Garlic, 4 cloves, minced

Chili powder, 4 tablespoons (1 oz/30 g)

Salt and freshly ground pepper

Crushed plum (Roma) tomatoes, 1 can (14½ oz/ 455 g)

Kidney or pinto beans, 2 cans (15 oz/470 g each), drained and rinsed

Chicken broth, 1 cup (8 fl oz/250 ml)

Sour cream, ½ cup (4 oz/ 125 g)

SERVES 4–6

roasted squash & bacon pasta

Butternut or other winter squash, 2 lb (1 kg), peeled, seeded, and cut into small cubes

Yellow onion, 1 large, halved and thinly sliced

Thick-cut bacon, 4 strips, cut into ½-inch (12-mm) pieces

Olive oil, 2 tablespoons

Fresh sage, 1 tablespoon finely chopped

Salt and freshly ground pepper

Rigatoni or other large pasta shape, 1 lb (500 g)

Parmesan cheese, ½ cup (2 oz/60 g) freshly grated, plus more for serving

SERVES 4

1 Roast the squash and onions

Preheat the oven to 425°F (220°C). On a large nonstick baking sheet, toss the squash, onion, and bacon with the oil. Sprinkle with the sage and season with salt and pepper. Spread in a single layer. Roast until the squash is caramelized and tender and the bacon is crispy, 15–20 minutes. Remove from the oven and set aside.

2 Cook the pasta

Meanwhile, bring a large pot of water to a boil. Add 2 tablespoons salt and the pasta to the boiling water. Cook, stirring occasionally to prevent sticking, until al dente, according to the package directions. Drain, reserving about ½ cup (4 fl oz/125 ml) of the cooking water. Return the pasta to the pot. Add the squash and onion and toss for 1 minute over high heat, adding as much of the cooking water as needed to loosen the sauce. Add the Parmesan, toss, and serve. Pass the additional Parmesan at the table.

cook's tip

For a delicious, homemade coleslaw to accompany the sandwiches, mix together ⅓ cup (3 fl oz/80 ml) mayonnaise, 2 tablespoons apple cider vinegar, 1 tablespoon Dijon mustard, and ½ head green cabbage, shredded. Toss well to combine and let stand for up to 20 minutes until the flavors have come together and the cabbage has wilted slightly.

bbq beef sandwiches

1 Cook the beef

In a large frying pan over medium-high heat, warm the oil. Add the onion and garlic and sauté until softened, about 5 minutes. Add the beef, season with salt and pepper, and cook until browned, stirring to break up any clumps, about 8 minutes. Add the barbecue sauce, reduce the heat to low, and cook until the meat is well coated and the sauce is heated through, about 5 minutes longer.

2 Assemble the sandwiches

Lightly toast the rolls. Place the open rolls on individual plates. Spoon the beef on the bottom half of each roll, set the top half in place, and serve.

Olive oil, 2 tablespoons

Yellow onion, 1 large, chopped

Garlic, 3 large cloves, minced

Ground (minced) beef, 1 1/2 lb (750 g)

Salt and freshly ground pepper

Barbecue sauce, 1 1/2 cups (12 fl oz/375 ml), purchased

Crusty sandwich rolls, 4, cut in half

SERVES 4

15 minutes
hands-on time

hungarian
beef stew

Olive oil, 2 tablespoons

Boneless beef chuck, 2 lb (1 kg), trimmed of excess fat and cut into 1½-inch (4-cm) pieces

Yellow onions, 2 large, chopped

Salt and freshly ground pepper

Garlic, 3 large cloves, minced

Sweet smoked paprika, 1½ tablespoons

Tomato paste, 2 tablespoons

Chicken broth, 4 cups (32 fl oz/1 l)

Boiling potatoes, 1 lb (500 g), quartered

Red bell pepper (capsicum), 1, seeded and cut into ½-inch (12-mm) strips

Carrots, 2, peeled and cut into 1-inch (12-mm) chunks

SERVES 4–6

1 Cook the onions and beef

In a Dutch oven over high heat, warm the oil. Add the beef and onions, season with salt and pepper, and cook, stirring frequently, until the beef is browned and the onions begin to caramelize, about 10 minutes. Stir in the garlic, paprika, and tomato paste. Add the broth, bring to a boil, reduce the heat to low, cover, and braise until the meat is nearly fork-tender, about 1 hour.

2 Finish the stew

Add the potatoes, bell pepper, and carrots, and continue to braise, covered, until the vegetables are tender, about 30 minutes longer. Divide the stew among individual shallow bowls and serve.

cook's tip

There are many different varieties
of Paprika, so be sure to use
a good-quality brand. Hungarian
and Spanish paprika are the most
popular, in particular Pimenton
de la Vera. These varieties come
in *dulce* (sweet) and *picante*
(spicy). For this recipe, use sweet
paprika or a combination
of sweet and spicy.

cook's tip

For an easy side dish, cook egg
noodles or another pasta shape
until al dente, according to the
package directions. Toss the pasta
with a little butter and chopped
fresh flat-leaf (Italian) parsley.

baked chicken parmesan

1 Brown the chicken

Preheat the oven to 400°F (200°C). Season the chicken generously with salt and pepper. In a large ovenproof frying pan over medium-high heat, warm the oil. Add the chicken and cook, turning once, until golden brown, about 7 minutes total. Transfer to a plate and set aside.

2 Bake the chicken

Add the kale to the frying pan and sauté over medium-high heat until wilted, about 1 minute. Add the chicken back to the frying pan with the kale and pour the marinara sauce over the chicken. Place 2 mozzarella slices on each chicken breast. Sprinkle evenly with the Parmesan cheese. Bake until the cheese is golden and the chicken is opaque throughout, about 20 minutes, then serve.

Skinless, boneless chicken breast halves, 4, about 1 ½ lb (750 g) total weight

Salt and freshly ground pepper

Olive oil, 2 tablespoons

Kale, 1 bunch, leaves stripped from stems and torn into large pieces

Marinara sauce, 2 cups (16 fl oz/500 ml), homemade or purchased, warmed

Fresh mozzarella cheese, 8 slices, ¼ inch (6 mm) thick

Parmesan cheese, ½ cup (2 oz/60 g) freshly grated

SERVES 4

vegetable enchiladas

Corn tortillas, 15, each 8 inches (20 cm) in diameter, halved

Canola oil, 2 tablespoons

Salt

Monterey jack cheese, 1 cup (4 oz/125 g) shredded

White Cheddar cheese, 1 cup (4 oz/125 g) shredded

Corn kernels, 2 cups (12 oz/370 g) fresh or frozen

Zucchini (courgettes), 2, halved lengthwise and thinly sliced

Yellow onion, 1 large, halved and thinly sliced

Tomatillo salsa, 2 jars (12½ oz/390 g each), ½ jar reserved for serving

Sour cream or Mexican *crema*, ¼ cup (2 oz/60 g)

***Queso fresco* or feta cheese,** ½ cup (2½ oz/75 g) crumbled

SERVES 4–6

1 **Toast the tortillas**
Preheat the oven to 400°F (200°C). Brush the tortillas with the oil, sprinkle with salt, and arrange on a baking sheet. Bake until crisp, 3–4 minutes. Remove from the oven and reduce the oven temperature to 300°F (150°C). In a small bowl, stir together the Monterey jack and Cheddar cheeses, corn, zucchini, and onion.

2 **Assemble the enchiladas**
Reserve ½ jar of the salsa for serving. Cover the bottom of a 9-inch (23-cm) round baking dish with a thin layer of salsa. Lay 10 tortilla halves over the salsa, overlapping if necessary. Top with one-fourth of the salsa and one-third of the cheese mixture, spreading them evenly. Repeat the layers two more times. Top the final layer of cheese mixture with the remaining salsa. Spoon the sour cream evenly over the top, then sprinkle with the *queso fresco*.

3 **Bake the enchiladas**
Cover the dish with aluminum foil and bake until the vegetables are tender and the cheese has melted, about 20 minutes. Uncover and continue to bake until the cheese is golden, 10–15 minutes longer. Let stand briefly before serving. Pass the remaining salsa at the table.

cook's tip

For chicken enchiladas, add
4 cups (1½ lb/750 g) cooked,
shredded meat to the enchiladas.
Remove and discard the skin
from purchased rotisserie chicken,
then pull the meat from the
bones. Shred the meat and add
to the cheese mixture in Step 1.

cook's tip

For a topping alternative, use thawed purchased puff pastry dough. Preheat the oven to 425°F (220°C) and lay the dough on top of the

filling in the dish. Trim the dough around the dish, leaving a 1-inch (2.5-cm) overhang. Fold the overhang back over itself and press it into the sides of the dish to make a sturdy rim. Prick the dough with a fork to create steam vents and bake until golden brown.

chicken
& leek pie

1 Prepare the filling

Preheat the oven to 375°F (190°C). In a large ovenproof frying pan over medium-high heat, melt the 4 tablespoons butter. Add the leeks, season with salt and pepper, and sauté until softened, about 5 minutes. Add the ⅓ cup flour and cook, stirring, for 2 minutes. Stir in the wine and broth and bring to a boil. Reduce the heat to low and simmer, stirring occasionally, until the liquid thickens slightly, about 5 minutes. Stir in the chicken and peas and season with salt and pepper.

2 Make the topping and bake the pie

In a bowl, combine the remaining flour, the baking powder, and ½ teaspoon salt. Using a pastry blender or 2 knives, cut in the 5 tablespoons butter until the mixture forms coarse crumbs about the size of peas. Add the milk and, using a rubber spatula, stir until evenly moistened. Place heaping spoonfuls of the batter evenly over the chicken filling. Bake until the topping is golden brown and the filling is bubbling, about 25 minutes.

Unsalted butter,
4 tablespoons (2 oz/60 g), plus 5 tablespoons (2½ oz/ 75 g)

Leeks, 2 large, white and pale green parts only, thinly sliced

Salt and freshly ground pepper

Flour, ⅓ cup (2 oz/60 g), plus 2 cups (10 oz/315 g)

Dry white wine, ¼ cup (2 fl oz/60 ml)

Chicken broth, 4 cups (32 fl oz/1 l)

Cooked chicken,
about 4 cups (1½ lb/750 g) shredded, homemade or purchased

Baby peas, 1 cup (5 oz/ 155 g)

Baking powder, 4 teaspoons

Milk, 1½ cups (12 fl oz/ 375 ml)

SERVES 4–6

mexican
pork pie

Boneless pork shoulder,
2½ lb (1.25 kg), cut into
1-inch (2.5-cm) pieces

Salt

Garlic, 4 cloves, minced

Chili powder, 3 tablespoons

Chicken broth, 2 cups
(16 fl oz/500 ml), plus
2½ cups (20 fl oz/625 ml)

**Crushed plum (Roma)
tomatoes,** 1 can (14½ oz/
455 g)

Dried oregano, 1 teaspoon
crumbled

Quick-cooking polenta,
1 cup (7 oz/220 g)

SERVES 6

1 Simmer the pork
Generously season the pork with salt. In an ovenproof
sauté pan over high heat, cook the pork, stirring frequently,
until browned, about 5 minutes. Add the garlic and 6 cups
(48 fl oz/1.5 l) water. Bring to a boil, reduce the heat to low,
and simmer, uncovered, until most of the water has evaporated,
1½–2 hours.

2 Cook the filling
Preheat the oven to 350ºF (180ºC). Raise the heat
to medium-high, sprinkle the pork with the chili powder and
cook, stirring, for about 1 minute. Add the 2 cups broth, the
tomatoes, and the oregano and simmer until the flavors are
blended, 2–3 minutes.

3 Make the polenta and finish the pie
In a saucepan over high heat, bring the 2½ cups broth
to a boil. Whisk in the polenta and 1 teaspoon salt. Reduce the
heat to low and cook, stirring frequently, until the polenta
is thick and creamy, about 5 minutes. Spoon over the top of the
pork. Bake until the polenta is browned, about 15 minutes.

cook's tip

If you prefer, top the pie with corn bread batter instead of quick-cooking polenta. To make corn bread, mix together 1 cup (5 oz/ 155 g) cornmeal, 1 cup (5 oz/ 155 g) flour, 2 tablespoons sugar, 1 teaspoon baking powder, ½ teaspoon salt. Stir in 1 cup milk (8 fl oz/250 ml) and 1 beaten egg. Bake for 15 minutes longer in Step 3, or until golden brown.

braised
short ribs

1 Brown the ribs
Preheat the oven to 325°F (165°C). Generously season the ribs with salt and pepper. In a Dutch oven or large ovenproof sauté pan over high heat, warm the oil. Working in batches if necessary, add the ribs, and cook, turning once, until browned, 8–10 minutes. Transfer the ribs to a plate.

2 Braise the ribs
Add the onion to the pot and sauté until softened, 2–3 minutes. Add the wine and port and cook, scraping up any brown bits from the pan bottom, 2–3 minutes. Return the ribs with any accumulated juices to the pot, and add enough broth so that it comes one-third of the way up the ribs. Bring to a boil and remove from the heat. Cover the pot tightly with aluminum foil, place the lid on the pot, and braise until the meat is fork-tender, 1½–2 hours. Add the potatoes and carrots and cook, covered, until the vegetables are tender, about 30 minutes longer.

3 Finish the dish
Using a slotted spoon, divide the ribs and vegetables among individual shallow bowls. Skim the fat from the sauce. Spoon some of the sauce over the ribs, garnish with the parsley, and serve.

Beef short ribs, 4–5 lb (2–2.5 kg) total weight, cut into 3 inch (7.5 cm) pieces

Salt and freshly ground pepper

Olive oil, 3 tablespoons

Yellow onion, 1, finely chopped

Dry red wine, 2 cups (16 fl oz/500 ml)

Port or brandy, 1 cup (8 fl oz/250 ml)

Chicken broth, 2 cups (16 fl oz/500 ml), plus more as needed

Boiling potatoes, 1 lb (500 g), quartered

Carrots, 2, cut into large chunks

Fresh flat-leaf (Italian) parsley, 2 tablespoons minced

SERVES 4–6

root vegetable pot pie

Frozen puff pastry, 1 sheet, thawed

Carrots, 2, cut into 1-inch (2.5-cm) chunks

Yellow onion, 1 large, chopped

Sweet potato, 1, peeled and cut into 1-inch (2.5-cm) chunks

Parsnips, 2, cut into 1-inch (2.5-cm) chunks

Fresh thyme, 4 sprigs, plus 1 tablespoon leaves

Olive oil, ¼ cup (2 fl oz/ 60 ml)

Salt and freshly ground pepper

Unsalted butter, 4 tablespoons (2 oz/60 g)

Flour, ¼ cup (1½ oz/45 g)

Dry white wine, ½ cup (4 fl oz/125 ml)

Vegetable broth, 2½ cups (20 fl oz/625 ml)

SERVES 4–6

1 Roast the vegetables

Preheat the oven to 400°F (200°C). On a floured work surface, roll the puff pastry to fit a 2-qt (1-l) baking dish. Place the pastry on a sheet of parchment (baking) paper and chill in the refrigerator. In the baking dish, toss the carrots, onion, sweet potato, parsnips, and thyme sprigs with the oil. Season with salt and pepper. Spread in an even layer and roast until the vegetables are tender, about 25 minutes.

2 Make the sauce

Meanwhile, in a small saucepan over medium-high heat, melt the butter. Add the flour, whisking constantly to prevent lumps from forming, and cook for 2 minutes. Add the wine and cook for 1 minute longer. Stir in the broth and bring to a boil. Stir in the thyme leaves.

3 Bake the pot pie

Remove the thyme sprigs from the roasted vegetables, and discard. Pour the sauce over the vegetables and toss well. Season with salt and pepper. Remove the pastry from the refrigerator and carefully fit on top of the vegetables. Bake until the pastry is golden and puffed and the filling is bubbling, 10–12 minutes. Serve directly from the pan.

cook's tip

You can easily vary the root vegetables in this delicious dish. Shop at a farmers market for the best selection of rutabagas, potatoes, turnips, and other seasonal root vegetables. The total should be a heaping 6 cups (30 oz/940 g).

cook's tip

Use this polenta pizza crust as
a base for a traditional Margherita
pizza. Spread a layer of tomato
sauce over the crust, top with
slices of fresh mozzarella cheese,
and sprinkle with sliced basil.

polenta pizza with tomatoes & ricotta

1 Make the polenta

Preheat the oven to 300°F (150°C). Coat a 9-inch (23-cm) round cake pan with oil. In a saucepan over high heat, bring 2½ cups (20 fl oz/625 ml) water to a boil. Whisk in the polenta and ½ teaspoon salt. Reduce the heat to low and cook, stirring frequently, until the polenta is thick and creamy, about 5 minutes. Remove from the heat and stir in the grated Parmesan.

2 Assemble the pizza

Spread the polenta in the prepared pan and drizzle with the oil. Bake until set in the center, about 15 minutes. Remove from the oven, spread the ricotta evenly over the polenta, top with the tomato slices, and sprinkle with salt.

3 Bake the pizza

Bake the pizza until the outside edge is golden brown, 10–15 minutes. Let cool briefly, sprinkle with the Parmesan shavings and basil, cut into wedges, and serve.

Quick-cooking polenta, 1 cup (7 oz/220 g)

Salt and freshly ground pepper

Parmesan cheese, ½ cup (2 oz/60 g) freshly grated, plus ½ cup (2 oz/60 g) shavings

Olive oil, 2 tablespoons

Ricotta cheese, 6 oz (185 g)

Tomatoes, 2 large, cut into thick slices

Fresh basil, 10 leaves, thinly sliced

SERVES 4

spiced
chicken & rice

Canola oil, 3 tablespoons

Skinless, boneless chicken breasts, 1½ lb (750 g), cut into 1-inch (2.5-cm) pieces

Salt and freshly ground pepper

Fresh ginger, 2 tablespoons minced

Curry powder, 1½ teaspoons

Chicken broth, 2½ cups (20 fl oz/625 ml)

Long-grain rice such as basmati, 1 cup (7 oz/220 g)

Golden raisins (sultanas), ¼ cup (1½ oz/45 g)

Finely grated zest and juice, from 1 lemon

Frozen baby peas, 1 cup (5 oz/155 g), thawed

Fresh cilantro (fresh coriander), ½ cup (¾ oz/ 20 g) minced

Roasted cashews, ½ cup (3 oz/90 g), coarsely chopped

SERVES 4–6

1 **Brown the chicken**
In a large Dutch oven over medium-high heat, warm the oil. Add the chicken, season with salt and pepper, and sauté, until browned on all sides, about 4 minutes. Transfer the chicken to a plate.

2 **Make the rice**
Add the ginger and curry powder to the pot and cook, stirring until fragrant, about 30 seconds. Stir in the broth, scraping up any browned bits from the pan bottom. Bring to a boil. Add the rice, raisins, lemon juice and zest, and 1 teaspoon salt. Return the chicken and any accumulated juices to the pot. Bring to a boil, reduce the heat to medium, cover, and cook until the rice is tender and the chicken is opaque throughout, about 20 minutes. Add the peas, cover, and let stand, for about 10 minutes. Sprinkle the cilantro and cashews over the rice, stir to combine, and serve.

cook's tip

Top with ½ cup (2 oz/60 g)
sweetened, shredded, dried
coconut that has been toasted
to enhance its nutty flavor.
To toast coconut, spread on
a baking sheet and place
in a preheated 350°F (180°C)
oven until light golden brown,
8–10 minutes.

cook's tip

To slice potatoes thinly, use the
slicer attachment on your food
processor. Or, use a mandoline
to achieve a similar result.

potato-cauliflower gratin

1 Cook the cauliflower

Preheat the oven to 400°F (200°C). Butter a 2-qt (2-l) baking dish. In a saucepan over high heat, combine the cream, garlic, thyme, 1 teaspoon salt, and ¼ teaspoon pepper. Bring to a boil, add the cauliflower, reduce the heat to low, and simmer until the cauliflower is just tender and the sauce has thickened, 8–10 minutes. Remove the garlic and thyme and discard.

2 Assemble and bake the gratin

Layer the potatoes in the prepared dish and sprinkle evenly with ½ cup *each* of the Gruyère and Parmesan cheeses. Using a slotted spoon, remove the cauliflower from the sauce and arrange in the dish. Top with the remaining cheeses. Pour the sauce evenly over the vegetables and sprinkle with the bread crumbs. Bake until the potatoes are just tender and the top is golden brown about 30 minutes. Let cool about 5 minutes before serving.

Heavy (double) cream, 2 cups (16 fl oz/500 ml)

Garlic, 3 cloves, crushed

Fresh thyme, 2 sprigs

Salt and freshly ground pepper

Cauliflower, 1 small head, separated into florets

Yukon gold potatoes, 2 lb (1 kg), peeled and thinly sliced

Gruyère cheese, 2 cups shredded (8 oz/250 g))

Parmesan cheese, 1 cup (4 oz/125 g) freshly grated

Fresh bread crumbs, ¼ cup (½ oz/15 g)

SERVES 4–6

67

baked ziti with prosciutto & peas

Salt

Ziti, penne or other tubular pasta, 1 lb (500 g)

Unsalted butter, ½ cup (4 oz/125 g)

Flour, ½ cup (2½ oz/75 g)

Milk, 4 cups (32 fl oz/1 l)

Nutmeg, ⅛ teaspoon freshly grated

Parmesan cheese, 2 cups (8 oz/250 g) freshly grated

Frozen baby peas, 1 cup (5 oz/155 g)

Prosciutto or ham, ¼ lb (125 g), chopped

Fresh bread crumbs, ½ cup (1 oz/30 g)

SERVES 4–6

1 Cook the pasta
Preheat the oven to 425°F (220°C) and butter a 2-qt (2-l) baking dish. Bring a large pot of water to a boil. Add 2 tablespoons salt and the pasta to the boiling water and cook, stirring occasionally to prevent sticking, until not quite al dente, about 2 minutes less than the package directions. Drain, rinse under cold running water, and set aside.

2 Make the sauce
In the same pot over medium heat, melt the butter. Add the flour and cook, stirring constantly, for 30 seconds. Gradually add the milk, whisking constantly to prevent lumps from forming, and cook until the sauce is thick and creamy, 5–10 minutes. Stir in the nutmeg, cheese, peas, and prosciutto. Return the pasta to the sauce and toss to combine.

3 Bake the pasta
Transfer the pasta and sauce to the prepared dish. Sprinkle with the bread crumbs. Bake until the bread crumbs are golden and the sauce is bubbling, about 20 minutes. Let cool for 10 minutes before serving.

cook's tip

Baked pasta dishes are always a crowd pleaser but you can save time by simply mixing the pasta with the hot sauce and then serving.

Omit the crumbs or garnish the pasta with toasted bread crumbs. Nearly any shaped pasta, such as linguine or bow-tie, can be used with this creamy, rustic sauce.

cook's tip

Make a vegetarian version
by omitting the pork and adding
vegetables such as shredded
red cabbage and thinly sliced
celery or cubed tofu. Add
to the vegetables in Step 2.

mu shu pork stir-fry

1 Marinate the pork

Preheat the oven to 400°F (200°C). In a small bowl, stir together the ⅓ cup hoisin sauce and the soy sauce. Add the pork, stir to coat, and set aside.

2 Cook the vegetables

In a large frying pan or wok over high heat, warm the oil. Add the cabbage, mushrooms, green onions, carrots, and water chestnuts and stir-fry until the vegetables are tender, 4–5 minutes. Add the ginger and stir-fry for 30 seconds. Add the pork and any remaining marinade and stir-fry until lightly browned, 2–3 minutes. Stir in the cornstarch mixture and cook, stirring often, until the sauce is thickened and the pork is opaque throughout, 2–3 minutes. Serve, passing the tortillas and hoisin sauce at the table.

Hoisin sauce, ⅓ cup (3 fl oz/80 ml), plus more for serving

Soy sauce, 2 tablespoons

Boneless pork loin chops, 1 lb (500 g), cut into thin strips

Canola oil, 2 tablespoons

Savoy cabbage, 1 small head, halved, cored, and thinly sliced crosswise

Shiitake mushrooms, 6 oz (185 g), stems discarded and caps thinly sliced

Green (spring) onions, 4, white and pale green parts, thinly sliced

Carrots, 3, coarsely grated

Water chestnuts, 1 can (8 oz/250 g), sliced

Fresh ginger, 2 tablespoons minced

Cornstarch (cornflour), 2 tablespoons, mixed with 2–3 tablespoons water

Flour tortillas, 8, each 8 inches (20 cm) in diameter, warmed

SERVES 4–6

chicken posole

Olive oil, 2 tablespoons

Yellow onions, 2 large, finely chopped

Celery, 2 stalks, chopped

Serrano or jalapeño chile, 2, cored, seeded, and minced

Garlic, 2 cloves, minced

Whole chicken, 1, 3 lb (1.5 kg), cut into 10 serving pieces

Hominy, 2 cans (15 oz/ 470 g each), drained and rinsed

Chili powder, 2 tablespoons

Dried oregano, 1 teaspoon crumbled

Salt and freshly ground pepper

Green cabbage, ¼ head, cored and thinly sliced

SERVES 6

1 Cook the chicken

In a large pot over medium-high heat, warm the oil. Set aside ¼ cup (1 oz/30 g) of the chopped onions for serving. Add the remaining onions and the celery to the pot and sauté until softened, 4–5 minutes. Add the chiles and garlic and cook until fragrant, about 30 seconds. Add the chicken pieces and 4 cups (32 fl oz/1 l) water and bring to a boil. Reduce the heat to medium-low and simmer until the chicken is opaque throughout, about 1 hour.

2 Finish the soup

Add the hominy, chili powder, and oregano and simmer for 5–10 minutes. Season with salt and pepper. Divide the posole among individual shallow bowls. Top with the cabbage and reserved onion, and serve.

cook's tip

You can substitute mussels for
the clams, or use a combination
of both. The mussels should
be scrubbed and debearded
before cooking.

spanish paella

1 Cook the sausages and rice

In a large frying pan or paella pan over medium-high heat, warm the oil. Add the sausage slices and cook, turning occasionally, until browned on both sides, about 3 minutes. Add the onion, bell pepper, and garlic and sauté until softened, 3–4 minutes. Season with salt and pepper. Add the rice, crumble in the saffron (if using), and cook, stirring, until the grains are well coated, about 2 minutes. Pour the broth into the pan and stir in 1 ½ teaspoons salt. Bring to a boil, reduce the heat to low, cover, and cook until the rice has absorbed nearly all of the liquid, about 20 minutes.

2 Cook the shellfish

Press the clams, hinge side down, into the rice, discarding any that do not close to the touch. Spread the shrimp over the rice and top with the peas. Cover and cook until the shrimp are opaque and the clams have opened, about 5 minutes longer. Discard any unopened clams and serve.

Olive oil, 2 tablespoons

Spanish chorizo or other spicy smoked sausages, 1 lb (500 g), cut into slices ½ inch (12 mm) thick

Yellow onion, 1, chopped

Red bell pepper (capsicum), 1, seeded and chopped

Garlic, 3 cloves, minced

Salt and freshly ground pepper

Long-grain white rice such as basmati, 2 cups (14 oz/ 440 g)

Saffron threads, ½ teaspoon (optional)

Chicken broth, 4 cups (32 fl oz/1 l)

Small clams such as littleneck or Manilla, 1–2 lb (500 g–1 kg), scrubbed

Large shrimp (prawns), 1 lb (500 g), peeled and deveined

Frozen baby peas, 1 cup (5 oz/155 g)

SERVES 4–6

make more
to store

roasted pork with hoisin vegetables

ROASTED PORK

Boneless pork loin roast,
4–4½ lb (2–2.5 kg)

Salt and freshly ground pepper

Hoisin sauce, ¼ cup
(2 fl oz/60 ml)

Soy sauce, ¼ cup (2 fl oz/
60 ml)

Asian sesame oil,
1 tablespoon

Acorn squash, 2 small,
seeded, and cut into wedges

Red onions, 2, halved and
cut into wedges

SERVES 4

makes about 4 cups
(3½ lb/1.75 kg) shredded
or thinly sliced total

Easy to prepare, roasted pork is served with hoisin-seasoned vegetables the first night. The additional pork can be used in Asian-inspired lettuce wraps, chipotle tacos, or sandwiches with a Cuban flare.

1 Roast the pork
Preheat the oven to 450°F (230°C). Season the pork with salt and pepper. Place the pork fat side up, in a roasting pan just large enough to hold it. Pour 2–3 tablespoons of water around the pork and roast for 25 minutes. If the pan becomes dry, add another 2 tablespoons water.

2 Season the vegetables
Meanwhile, in a large bowl, stir together the hoisin sauce, soy sauce, and sesame oil. Add the squash and the onions and toss to coat.

3 Finish the pork
Reduce the oven temperature to 325°F (165°C). Baste the pork with the pan drippings, and arrange the vegetables around the pork. Continue to roast until an instant-read thermometer inserted into the center of the pork registers 145°–150°F (63°–65°C), and the pork is barely pink in the center, about 45–50 minutes longer. Transfer the pork to a carving board and let rest for 10 minutes. Slice enough pork for one meal and serve with the hoisin vegetables. Let the remaining pork cool, then store for later use (see Storage Tip, right).

storage tip

To store the roasted pork that
is not being served immediately,
enclose it, unsliced, in one
or two layers of plastic wrap and
refrigerate it for up to 4 days.

cook's tip

To prepare a mango, stand the mango on one of its narrow edges. Using a sharp knife, cut down along each side of the stem end, just grazing the pit. Peel each half using a vegetable peeler or paring knife. Then, cut each half into slices. Slice off any flesh clinging to the pit.

pork & mango lettuce wraps

1 Heat the pork

In a large frying pan over medium-high heat, warm the oil. Add the chile and sauté until softened, about 1 minute. Add the pork, stir in the soy sauce, fish sauce, sugar, and garlic, and cook until the pork is heated through, about 1 minute longer. Remove from the heat and stir in the cilantro.

2 Assemble the wraps

Divide the pork mixture in the center of each lettuce leaf. Top with mango slices, sprinkle with peanuts, and serve.

Roasted Pork, 3 cups (1½ lb/750 g), cut into thin strips or shredded (page 78)

Peanut or canola oil, 2 tablespoons

Jalapeño or serrano chile, 1, cored, seeded, and minced

Soy sauce, ¼ cup (2 fl oz/ 60 ml)

Asian fish sauce, 3 tablespoons

Sugar, 2 tablespoons

Garlic, 3 cloves, minced

Fresh cilantro (fresh coriander), 1 cup (1 oz/ 30 g) leaves

Iceberg lettuce, 8 large leaves

Mango, 1, peeled, pitted, and thinly sliced

Dry roasted peanuts, ½ cup (3 oz/90 g) chopped

SERVES 4

chipotle
pork tacos

Roasted Pork, 3 cups
(1½ lb/750 g), cut into thin
strips, or shredded (page 78)

Olive oil, 3 tablespoons

**Salt and freshly ground
pepper**

**Chipotle chiles in adobo
sauce,** 1 can (7 oz/199 g)

Juice of 1 lime

Corn tortillas, 8, each
5 inches (13 cm) in diameter,
warmed

Avocado, 1, halved, pitted,
peeled, and thinly sliced

**Fresh cilantro (fresh
coriander),** ½ cup (½ oz/
15 g) leaves

Red onion, ¼, minced

Queso fresco, ½ cup
(2½ oz/75 g), crumbled

SERVES 4

1 **Heat the pork**
In a large frying pan over medium-high heat, warm
2 tablespoons of the oil. Add the pork, season with salt and
pepper, and cook until heated through, about 2 minutes.

2 **Make the salsa and assemble the tacos**
In a blender, purée the chipotle chiles in adobo sauce,
the remaining 1 tablespoon oil, and the lime juice. Divide the
pork evenly among the tortillas. Drizzle with the salsa and top
with the avocado. Garnish with cilantro, onion, and *queso
fresco*, and serve.

82

cook's tip

The versatile chipotle salsa
can be made up to 1 week
in advance and stored in
an airtight container. Serve
as a condiment for grilled
chicken or for scrambled eggs
on toasted country bread.

cook's tip

The sandwiches can also be made
on a split baguette or rustic loaf
such as ciabatta. After layering
the ingredients in the loaf, cut
into 4 individual sandwiches,
and serve.

cuban pork sandwich

1 Assemble the sandwiches

Preheat a heavy frying pan or grill pan over medium-high heat. Spread the bottom of each roll with mustard. Layer the pork, ham, cheese, and pickles on the rolls, dividing evenly. Set the top halves in place and press gently. Brush the tops of the rolls with the melted butter.

2 Grill the sandwiches

Place the sandwiches in the heated pan and weight with a second pan. Grill until the undersides are golden, about 2½ minutes. Turn the sandwiches, weight again, and cook until the other sides are golden and the cheese is melted, about 2½ minutes longer.

Roasted Pork, 2 cups (1 lb/ 500 g), thinly sliced (page 78)

Crusty rolls such as Portuguese rolls, 4, split horizontally

Dijon mustard, 4 teaspoons

Smoked ham or Genoa salami, 1 lb (500 g), thinly sliced

Swiss cheese, ½ lb (250 g), thinly sliced

Dill pickle slices, ½ cup (2 oz/60 g)

Unsalted butter, 2 tablespoons, melted

SERVES 4

braised chicken & vegetables

BRAISED CHICKEN

Whole chickens, 2, about 3½ lb (1.75 kg) each, neck and giblets removed, cut into 16 serving pieces

Flour, ½ cup (2½ oz/75 g)

Salt and freshly ground pepper

Unsalted butter, 4 tablespoons (2 oz/60 g)

Dry red wine, 2 cups (16 fl oz/500 ml)

Chicken broth, 2 cups (16 fl oz/500 ml)

Diced tomatoes, 1 can (14½ oz/455 g) with juice

Fresh thyme, 3 sprigs

Button mushrooms, ½ lb (250 g), halved

Carrots, 1 lb (500 g), cut into 2-inch (5-cm) pieces

SERVES 4

makes about 8 cups (3 lb/1.5 kg) shredded cooked chicken total

Browning the chicken before braising it ensures moist, flavorful meat. Serve it with vegetables the first night, and use the leftovers in a light soup, a baguette sandwich, or a hearty pasta sauce.

1 **Brown the chicken**
In a shallow bowl, combine the flour, 1½ teaspoons salt, and ½ teaspoon pepper. Dredge the chicken pieces in the flour mixture, shaking off any excess. In a large frying pan over medium-high heat, melt the butter. Working in batches, add the chicken and cook, turning once or twice, until golden brown, about 8 minutes. Transfer the chicken to a plate.

2 **Make the sauce**
Pour the wine in the pan and cook over medium-high heat for about 2 minutes, scraping up any browned bits on the bottom of the pan. Add the broth, tomatoes, and thyme. Bring to a boil, reduce the heat to low, and simmer to reduce the liquid, about 5 minutes. Return the chicken and any accumulated juices to the pan. Add the mushrooms and carrots, cover, and braise until the vegetables are tender and the chicken is opaque throughout, 25–30 minutes. Remove 8 pieces of chicken and let to cool before storing (see Storage Tip, right). Divide the remaining chicken and vegetables among shallow bowls, top with the sauce, and serve.

storage tip

To store the chicken, let it cool,
then remove the meat from
the bones. Discard the skin and
bones. Shred the meat and
put in an airtight container or
resealable plastic bag. Store
the chicken in the refrigerator
for up to 3 days.

cook's tip

If you cannot find Swiss chard, you can use 6 oz (185 g) baby spinach. Remove the stems, rinse the leaves, dry completely, and then chop.

chicken &
vegetable soup

1 Sauté the vegetables
In a large saucepan over medium heat, warm the oil.
Add the carrots, onion, and celery, season with salt and pepper,
and sauté until softened, about 5 minutes. Add the chicken
broth, increase the heat to medium-high, and bring to a boil.

2 Cook the pasta
Add the pasta and the chicken to the pan and return
to a boil. Cook, stirring often, until the pasta is not quite al dente,
about 3 minutes. Stir in the chard and cook until wilted, about
1 minute. Season with salt and pepper. Ladle the soup into
bowls and serve. Pass the Parmesan at the table.

Braised Chicken, 2 cups
(12 oz/375 g) shredded
(page 86)

Olive oil, 2 tablespoons

Carrots, 2, finely chopped

Yellow onion, 1 large, finely
chopped

Celery, 1 stalk, finely chopped

**Salt and freshly ground
pepper**

Chicken broth, 6 cups
(48 fl oz/1.5 l)

**Conchiglie or other small
pasta shape,** 1 cup (3½ oz/
105 g)

Swiss chard, 1 bunch, ribs
removed, leaves cut crosswise
into thin strips

Parmesan cheese, ¼ cup
(2 oz/60 g) freshly grated

SERVES 4

chicken sandwiches with peppers

Braised Chicken, 2 cups
(12 oz/375 g) shredded
(page 86)

Baguette, 1, about 24 inches
(60 cm) split horizontally

Olive oil, ¼ cup (2 fl oz/
60 ml)

**Red bell pepper
(capsicum),** 1, seeded and
thinly sliced

Yellow onion, 1 large, thinly
sliced

Garlic, 2 cloves, minced

**Salt and freshly ground
pepper**

Provolone cheese, 8 slices

SERVES 4

1 **Toast the bread**
Preheat the broiler (grill). Open the baguette and place
on a baking sheet. Broil until lightly toasted. Cut into 4 equal
lengths, and set aside.

2 **Sauté the vegetables**
In a large frying pan over high heat, warm the oil. Add
the bell pepper and onion and sauté until softened and slightly
caramelized, about 10 minutes. Add the garlic and cook until
fragrant, about 1 minute. Add the chicken and stir until heated
through, 2–3 minutes. Season with salt and pepper.

3 **Assemble the sandwiches**
Divide the chicken mixture evenly among the bottom
of the toasted baguette pieces and top with the cheese. Place
the filled bottom halves of the sandwiches on the baking sheet
and broil until the cheese is melted, about 1 minute. Transfer
to individual plates, top with the other baguette half, and serve.

cook's tip

If desired, serve the sandwiches topped with heated marinara sauce. Look for a good-quality, jarred sauce at an Italian market or well-stocked supermarket.

cook's tip

Marsala is a fortified wine from Sicily that is appreciated for its distinctive, slightly sweet flavor. Sherry or any other fortified wine can be used in its place.

penne with chicken ragu

1 Prepare the sauce

Bring a large pot of water to a boil. In a large frying pan over medium-high heat, warm the oil. Add the carrots and onion, season with salt and pepper, and sauté until softened, about 5 minutes. Add the Marsala and cook until the alcohol has evaporated, about 2 minutes. Add the tomatoes with their juice and broth and bring to a boil. Reduce the heat to medium, stir in the chicken, and simmer until the sauce is thickened slightly, about 10 minutes.

2 Cook the pasta

Meanwhile, add 2 tablespoons salt and the pasta to the boiling water. Cook, stirring occasionally to prevent sticking, until the pasta is al dente, according to the package directions. Drain, reserving about ½ cup (4 fl oz/125 ml) of the cooking water. Add the pasta to the sauce and toss to combine. Warm briefly over low heat to blend the flavors. Add as much of the cooking water as needed to loosen the sauce. Serve, passing the Parmesan at the table.

Braised Chicken, 2 cups (12 oz/375 g) shredded (page 86)

Olive oil, 2 tablespoons

Carrots, 2, chopped

Yellow onion, 1, chopped

Salt and freshly ground pepper

Marsala, sherry, or other fortified wine, ½ cup (4 fl oz/125 ml)

Crushed plum (Roma) tomatoes, 1 can (14½ oz/ 455 g)

Chicken broth, 1 cup (8 fl oz/250 ml)

Penne or other tubular pasta, 1 lb (500 g)

Parmesan cheese, ½ cup (2 oz/60 g) freshly grated

SERVES 4

the smarter cook

When you want to put supper on the table quickly, there is no easier way to do it than to make a delicious one-pot meal. The recipes in this book are your key to serving simple yet inspired dishes even on busy weeknights. Use them to create a weekly meal plan that will allow you to spend less time shopping, preparing, and cleaning up and more time enjoying home-cooked meals with your family every night.

Keep your pantry well stocked and you'll have the foundation for one-pot meals all week long. Plan your menus in advance and you'll make fewer trips to the store. Cook two chickens on the weekend and use one of them for making other tasty recipes during the week. In the following pages, you'll find valuable tips like these on how to manage your time and stock your kitchen—the keys to becoming a smarter cook.

get started

With a little advance planning and a well-organized kitchen, you can become a smarter cook who turns out satisfying one-pot meals every night of the week. Easy strategies such as keeping a well-stocked pantry (page 104), putting together a weekly meal plan, and giving some thought to how cooking fits into your schedule will help you make the most of your time.

■ **Look at the whole week.** By looking at the week as a whole, you'll be able to vary your meals and make your menus interesting. Keep your schedule in mind as you plan. Put together at least one menu with a main dish that can be doubled easily, like the Braised Chicken & Vegetables on page 86, so you can use the leftovers as the base for a meal later in the week. Celebrations or even casual get-togethers with friends can be a good excuse for putting more festive dishes, like paella or a hearty gumbo, on the table. Mix up the menus so they offer a variety of cooking techniques and flavors throughout the week, with delicious Baked Chicken Parmesan (page 51) one night and Turkey Poblano Chili (page 41) the next.

■ **Let the seasons guide you.** Choose recipes that match the weather: hearty roasts, stews, and casseroles in the winter, and light pastas, sandwiches, and salads in the warmer months. Take advantage of the season's best fresh ingredients. You'll enjoy better flavors and you'll save money, too, because in-season foods are typically less expensive and always taste better.

■ **Plan for leftovers.** Make a simple recipe that has a big yield: roast a big pork loin or make a large stew or soup. It takes the about the same amount of cooking time as a smaller portion, and the leftovers are a great time-saver when you need a satisfying dish fast. Simply reheat leftovers or use them to make a new dish with new flavors.

■ **Get everyone involved.** Enlist kids and other family members in choosing the week's menus and they'll enjoy each meal more. Encourage them to help you with the preparation, too.

THINK SEASONALLY

Here is a guide to using the best that each season has to offer whenever you are making recipes in this book.

spring Serve light main courses, salads, soups, and pastas prepared with seasonal ingredients, such as asparagus, fennel, fresh herbs (dill, chives, parsley, and mint), green (spring) onions, new potatoes, peas, and lamb.

summer Focus on the best of the harvest, such as avocados, bell peppers (capsicums), chiles, corn, cucumbers, eggplants (aubergines), green beans, tomatoes, and zucchini (courgettes) or other summer squashes.

autumn Prepare stews, gratins, and pot pies made with the season's root vegetables and other ingredients, like leeks, butternut squash, cauliflower, potatoes, and yams.

winter Cook flavorful roasts, braises, or spicy curries with winter vegetables and other fresh seasonal ingredients, such as beets, cabbage, chard, fresh herbs (sage and rosemary), kale, wild and cultivated mushrooms, turnips, and winter squashes.

round it out

Once you have decided which recipe to make as the centerpiece of your meal, choose among a wide variety of appealing side dishes to round out the menu. Keep in mind both speed and ease of preparation.

steamed rice Use aromatic white or nutty brown rice to pair with stir-fries, curries, and braises. You can cook it in advance and refrigerate it in sealed plastic bags.

potatoes Bake russet or sweet potatoes for an easy, inexpensive partner to meat dishes. Russet and Yukon gold potatoes also mash well, making a delicious accompaniment to braises or stews. Toss fingerling or small red-skinned potatoes with olive oil, salt, pepper, and chopped fresh rosemary before roasting them.

whole grains Seek out whole-grain bulgur, quinoa, or other grains for nutritious, full-flavored side dishes. Sauté the grain in a little canola oil or butter until it releases a nutty fragrance. Add hot water or broth, cover tightly, and simmer until the grain is tender.

couscous Quick-cooking couscous, available flavored or plain, takes less than 10 minutes to prepare. While it is typically served hot, it is also good cold: toss it with minced green (spring) onions and drizzle with a light vinaigrette for an easy summer salad.

polenta Cook a double batch of instant polenta and serve half for dinner. Pour the remainder into a lightly oiled baking dish, let cool, cover, and refrigerate. Cut the polenta into triangles or squares and broil (grill) or panfry until browned on both sides.

salad Choose salad ingredients that complement your main dish: sliced cucumber and chopped fresh herbs drizzled with olive oil and red wine vinegar to go with paella, or arugula (rocket) and sliced radicchio with a balsamic vinaigrette to pair with an Italian dish. Make extra dressing and refrigerate for another meal.

tomatoes Slice fresh, ripe summer tomatoes and arrange on a platter. Just before serving, sprinkle with sea salt and pepper and drizzle with a fruity olive oil or an herbed aioli. If desired, tuck fresh basil leaves between the slices and top with thinly sliced, fresh mozzarella or crumbled feta cheese.

fresh vegetables You can steam, blanch, or roast many vegetables a day ahead, and then reheat them in a frying pan with a drizzle of olive oil or a pat of butter at dinnertime. Or, mix them with slivered almonds or fresh herbs, toss them with olive oil and lemon juice or a vinaigrette, and serve them at room temperature.

roasted vegetables Cauliflower, asparagus, and bell peppers (capsicums) are well suited to high-heat roasting. Toss them with olive oil, salt, and pepper and roast in a single layer on a baking sheet in a 425°F (220°C) oven, stirring occasionally, until tender and golden, 10–20 minutes. Peel and cube root vegetables and roast in a similar manner at 350°F (180°C).

cooked greens Sauté Swiss chard, spinach, or beet greens in a little olive oil. Shred or chop tougher greens, such as kale and collards, add a small amount of broth, cover, and cook, stirring often, until tender.

artisanal bread Warm a crusty French or Italian loaf and serve it with room-temperature butter or olive oil. To make garlic bread, mix melted butter with minced garlic to taste. Halve a baguette horizontally and brush with the garlic butter. Wrap in aluminum foil and place in a 300°F (150°C) oven until the bread is crisp and heated through.

sample menus

Here are some ideas on how to create a satisfying supper by adding side dishes to your one-pot recipe. IN MINUTES menus highlight recipes that go together quickly, WEEKEND suppers require more cooking time, and FIT FOR COMPANY meals feature especially festive main courses for a special get-together.

IN MINUTES	WEEKEND	FIT FOR COMPANY
BBQ Beef Sandwiches (page 45) Iceberg lettuce wedge with blue cheese dressing	**Roasted Pork with Hoisin Vegetables** (page 78) Steamed jasmine rice Stir-fried sugar snap peas	**Halibut with Tomatoes & Leeks** (page 21) Orzo pasta with lemon and olive oil Roasted asparagus
Creamy Mushroom Stroganoff (page 26) Mixed salad greens with balsamic vinaigrette	**Baked Ziti with Prosciutto & Peas** (page 68) Arugula (rocket) & Parmesan salad with balsamic vinaigrette Bread sticks	**Root Vegetable Pot Pie** (page 60) Sliced tomatoes with crumbled blue cheese Mixed salad greens with balsamic vinaigrette
Apricot-Glazed Chicken (page 22) Rice pilaf Roasted broccoli	**Pork Chops with Cider Glaze** (page 18) Mashed potatoes Steamed English peas	**Roasted Squash & Bacon Pasta** (page 42) Braised kale with pine nuts
Tortellini & Vegetable Soup (page 30) Butter lettuce with buttermilk dressing	**Herbed Sweet Potatoes with Feta** (page 10) Panfried Italian sausages Braised winter greens	**Mustard-Crusted Salmon & Potatoes** (page 37) Sautéed green beans with butter
Spinach & Cheese Stuffed Chicken (page 14) Sliced tomatoes with olive oil, salt, and pepper	**Spicy Steamed Clams** (page 33) Mixed salad greens with citrus vinaigrette Crusty garlic bread	**Spanish Paella** (page 75) Mixed salad greens with sherry vinaigrette Crusty bread
Broccoli & Pancetta Frittata (page 38) Roasted potato wedges		

Once you have planned your menus for the week, give some thought to the best way to organize your time. The more you can do in advance, the more quickly and easily the meal will come together at dinnertime.

shop less If you have made a weekly meal plan, you will probably need to shop only two or three times a week for fresh ingredients like produce or meat.

do it ahead Do as much as you can ahead of time. Some ingredients can be prepped in advance. For example, chop or slice vegetables or meats the night before or in the morning to save time at dinnertime. Pack them in separate containers and store in the refrigerator. Also, check the recipes for steps that can be done ahead, such as browning meat or making a salsa.

cook smarter Before you begin, take a few minutes to reread the recipe and to assemble your equipment and prep your ingredients. If possible, enlist family members to help you with assembly and cleanup.

double up When planning a week's worth of dinners, look for opportunities to utilize one night's leftovers, such as roasted pork, in other recipes like tacos, wraps, or sandwiches.

clean as you go Before you begin cooking, empty the dishwasher. To ensure an easy clean-up, Wash the pots and pans, and utensils as you cook, so that when you sit down to eat, the kitchen work surfaces are clear.

tools for success

■ **Baking sheets and pans.** Sometimes called jelly-roll pans, these large rectangular metal baking pans with shallow sides are especially handy for roasting vegetables. Look for heavy baking sheets to ensure foods cook more evenly and the metal doesn't warp in the high-heat oven. Baking pans and dishes made of tempered glass, porcelain, earthenware, or heavy-gauge aluminum are handy for everything from potpies to baked chicken.

■ **Roasting pan.** A rectangular roasting pan is indispensable for cooking large cuts of meat and poultry. Its relatively low sides allow the oven heat to reach most of the surface of the item being roasted. Look for a heavy stainless-steel, anodized-aluminum, or enameled-steel pan to ensure even heat distribution. Also, the heavier the pan, the less likely it will warp or dent. Opposing looped handles simplify getting the pan in and out of the oven.

■ **Frying pan.** Also known as a skillet, this broad, shallow pan has sides that flare outward and a long handle. Most home cooks should have two sizes, 9- or 10-inch (23- or 25-cm) and 12- or 14-inch (30- or 35-cm). If you are buying a frying pan, choose an ovenproof one made from castiron or anodized aluminum. For the recipes in this book, you'll also need a relatively deep, straight-sided frying pan, typically called a sauté pan, which comes with a lid.

■ **Dutch oven.** This large, round or oval pot with a tight-fitting lid and two loop handles is used for slow cooking on the stove top or in the oven. It is most commonly made from enameled cast iron and comes in sizes ranging from 4 to 12 quarts (4 to 12 l). A 6- to 8-quart (6- to 8-l) pot is recommended for most home kitchens.

■ **Cake pans.** A 9-inch (23-cm) round cake pan with 2-inch (5-cm) sides is handy for shaping a pizza crust made from quick-cooking polenta. You can also pour freshly cooked polenta into an oiled cake pan, let the polenta cool and set, and then cut it into wedges or squares for panfrying or broiling (grilling).

shop smarter

Using the freshest produce and other high-quality ingredients will help ensure great-tasting dinners and healthier eating. Seek out a butcher, fishmonger, produce store, and specialty-food shop that stock top-notch ingredients at reasonable prices and patronize them regularly. Call ahead and place your order, so it's ready to pick up on your way home from work.

■ **Produce** When you are at the market, ask which fruits and vegetables are at their peak of flavor and ripeness. If there is a regular farmers' market in your area, get in the habit of visiting it once a week. It's an excellent way to stay in touch with what is in season, and you'll often find good deals on bumper-crop produce. Choose vegetables and fruits that are free of bruises and blemishes and feel heavy for their size. Greens and herbs should be crisp and brightly colored, and vegetables such as eggplants (aubergines) and zucchini (courgettes) should have taut skins and be firm to the touch.

■ **Meat & poultry** Look for meat with good, uniform color and a fresh smell. Any fat should be bright white rather than grayish. Poultry should be plump, with smooth skin and firm flesh, and any visible fat should be white to light yellow. If you need boned meat or poultry, ask the butcher to do it for you, to save you time in the kitchen.

■ **Seafood** Look for fish and shellfish with bright color, a moist surface, and little or no "fishy" smell. Ask the purveyor which fish and shellfish are freshest. If possible, use seafood the same day you purchase it.

■ **Broth** Good-quality broths can be found in cans and aseptic boxes on market shelves. Read the labels carefully to avoid unwholesome ingredients and, if possible, purchase organic brands for both better health and flavor. Many specialty-food shops sell their own made-from-scratch fresh or frozen broths, which are another good option.

■ **Wine** Ask your wine merchant to recommend good everyday red and white wines at reasonable prices. Buy wine by the case, so you always have a supply on hand; you will often get a discount for buying in bulk.

TIME-SAVING TOOLS

food processor A miniprocessor is useful for chopping small amounts of herbs. A standard-sized processor with a 12- to 14-cup (3- to 3.5-l) capacity is handy for making pesto, chopping onions, grating cheese or carrots, and puréeing a wide variety of foods.

salad spinner Whether your spinner uses a pump, crank, or pull cord, the centrifugal force whirling salad greens will ensure a crisp, dry salad. A large-sized spinner is best for salad greens, while a smaller-sized spinner is ideal for washing and drying fresh herbs.

microplane Available in various sizes and degrees of fineness, these handheld, easy-to-use graters are unsurpassed for fast-and-easy grating of hard cheese, citrus zest, and fresh ginger.

bowls A set of small bowls in graduated sizes is helpful for readying your ingredients. Before you begin cooking, assemble and measure all the ingredients you need and put them in bowls. This helps avoid cluttered counters and searching the pantry for items at the last-minute. A set of larger bowls is useful for mixing ingredients.

Certain ingredients will make the job easier, save prep time, and sometimes add concentrated, intense flavor. Here are some items that are particularly useful when making one-pot meals.

rotisserie chicken Buy enough chicken for dinner one night plus leftovers, and cut up the leftover meat to add to a simple one-pot dish the next night. Add the chicken toward the end of the cooking time so that it won't toughen from overheating.

canned tomatoes Canned tomatoes don't need to be peeled, require a shorter cooking time, and are more flavorful than out-of-season tomatoes.

frozen puff pastry Making homemade dough is labor-intensive, which makes frozen puff pastry a handy alternative. Thaw the pastry in the refrigerator according to the package instructions, and keep it chilled until ready to use.

precooked sausages Slice fully cooked meat or poultry sausages, and add to a dish such as Tortellini and Vegetable Soup (page 30). Or, brown the sausages first for extra flavor and serve alongside such dishes such as Herbed Sweet Potatoes with Feta (page 10).

precut vegetables & fruit If you're pressed for time, supermarkets now stock a wide variety of prewashed, precut fruits and vegetables, that can come in handy for putting together last-minute salads or crudité or dessert platters.

easy techniques

Nothing will speed your time in the kitchen more than familiarity with a handful of everyday cooking techniques. With a little practice, you'll gather confidence in your culinary abilities and you'll shorten the time you spend at the stove.

■ **Sauté.** Sautéed foods are cooked quickly, usually over medium or medium-high heat, in a small amount of butter or oil. Be sure to dry any foods to be sautéed on paper towels before adding them to the pan, or the food will steam rather then sear. For the same reason, don't crowd the pan.

■ **Brown.** Browning meat or poultry before combining it with other ingredients in a recipe will impart a richer flavor and color to the finished dish. First, pat the food dry with paper towels to ensure a nice brown exterior. Then, add it to a little oil or butter in a frying pan or Dutch oven over medium-high heat and turn the pieces until richly colored on all sides. Never crowd the pan or the food won't brown properly, and use tongs or a slotted spoon to transfer the food to a plate, where it can remain until you are ready to combine it with the other ingredients. Be sure to include any accumulated juices on the plate for added flavor.

■ **Reduce.** Reducing a liquid by simmering or boiling concentrates its flavor and thickens its consistency by decreasing its quantity through evaporation. It's a handy sauce-making technique when preparing one-pot meals, since it can be done in the same pan in which the ingredients for the dish were cooked.

■ **Roast.** Roasting meats and poultry in an uncovered roasting pan in the oven intensifies their flavors. Because the oven does most of the work, it's a technique that requires little hands-on time. Line a heavy roasting pan with aluminum foil and brush the foil with a little olive oil to help prevent sticking.

■ **Season.** Remove a small amount of the finished dish from the pot, taste, season with salt and pepper, and taste again. This gives you an idea of how much seasoning to add, so you don't overseason the whole pot.

the well-stocked kitchen

Smart cooking is all about being prepared. If your pantry, refrigerator, and freezer are well stocked and organized, you'll always have a head start on making supper. And if you keep track of what is in your kitchen, you'll shop less often and you'll spend less time in the store when you do.

In the pages that follow, you'll find a guide to all of the ingredients you'll need to have on hand to make the recipes in this book, plus dozens of tips for keeping them fresh and storing them properly. Use the lists to find out what you already have in your kitchen and what you need to buy when you go shopping. The time you spend shopping and putting your kitchen in order will be time well spent—an investment in smarter cooking that pays off whenever you need to put dinner on the table.

the pantry

The pantry is typically a place in which you store dried herbs and spices, pasta and grains, canned goods, and such fresh ingredients as garlic, onions, shallots, and any root vegetables that don't require refrigeration. Make sure that it is a cool, dry, and dark place. It should also be a good distance from the stove, as heat can dry out certain pantry staples, especially spices, robbing them of their flavor.

stock your pantry

- Take inventory of what is in your pantry using the Pantry Staples list.

- Remove everything from the pantry; clean the shelves and reline with paper, if needed; and then resort the items by type.

- Discard items that have passed their expiration date or have a stale or otherwise questionable appearance.

- Make a list of items that you need to replace or stock.

- Shop for the items on your list.

- Restock the pantry, organizing items by type so everything is easy to find.

- Write the purchase date on perishable items and clearly label bulk items.

- Keep staples you use often toward the front of the pantry.

- Keep dried herbs and spices in their containers and preferably in a dedicated spice or herb organizer, shelf, or drawer.

keep it organized

- Look over the recipes in your weekly menu plan and check your pantry to make sure you have all the ingredients you'll need.

- Rotate items as you use them, moving the oldest ones to the front of the pantry so they will be used first.

- Keep a list of the items you use up so that you can replace them.

USING DRIED HERBS

Fresh herbs, with their bright taste, are generally the best choice for flavoring one-pot dishes, but some dried herbs can also be used successfully.

The flavor of dried herbs is concentrated, so always use a smaller amount of the dried herb than the fresh. For example:

1 teaspoon dried tarragon or sage = 1 tablespoon fresh

2 teaspoons dried oregano, marjoram, or thyme = 1 tablespoon fresh

1 ½ teaspoons dried rosemary = 1 tablespoon fresh

BUYING BROTH

Be careful when reducing commercial broths because many brands contain a lot of salt that will become more concentrated as the liquid evaporates. Always try to buy reduced-sodium broths to avoid this problem. Good-quality organic chicken, beef, and vegetable broths can be found in cans and aseptic boxes on market shelves.

PANTRY STORAGE

Keep pantry items in small quantities so you restock regularly, ensuring freshness.

dried herbs & spices Always store herbs and spices in a cool place away from direct heat, such as a stove top. Heat will cause them to dry out, losing their volatile oils that provide flavor. Even many properly dried seasonings lose potency after 6 months. Shop for herbs and spices in ethnic markets and natural-foods stores, where they are often sold in bulk and are usually cheaper and of higher quality.

oils Store unopened bottles of oil on a cool, dark shelf for up to 1 year. Once opened, store at room temperature for 3 months or in the refrigerator for as long as 6 months. Smell oil before using to make sure it has not developed an off odor, which can be a sign of rancidity.

grains & pastas Store grains and pastas in airtight containers. Grains will keep for up to 3 months; unopened pastas will keep for up to 1 year. Once opened, use pasta within 6 months.

fresh foods Store in a cool, dark place and check occasionally for sprouting or spoilage. Keep potatoes in a loosely closed paper bag to shield them from direct light, which can cause their skins to turn green.

canned foods Discard canned foods if the can shows any signs of buckling or expansion. Once you have opened a can, transfer unused contents to an airtight container and store in the refrigerator or freezer.

PANTRY STAPLES

OILS
Asian sesame oil

olive oil

peanut oil

VINEGARS
cider vinegar

red wine vinegar

CANNED & JARRED FOODS
apricot jam

Asian fish sauce

chicken broth

chipotle chiles in adobo sauce

coconut milk, unsweetened

curry paste, Thai green

Dijon mustard

hoisin sauce

tomatillo salsa

tomatoes

soy sauce

white beans, such as cannellini

PASTA & GRAINS
couscous

dried pasta such as penne

egg noodles

long-grain white rice

quick-cooking polenta

WINES & SPIRITS
dry white wine

dry red wine

Marsala

port

DRIED HERBS & SPICES
chili powder

curry powder

dried oregano

dry mustard

Old Bay or crab boil seasoning

paprika, sweet

red pepper flakes

saffron threads

MISCELLANEOUS
apple cider

cashews, roasted

cornstarch

flour

golden raisins (sultanas)

panko or dried bread crumbs

pine nuts

tortillas, corn and flour

FRESH FOODS
garlic

ginger

lemons

leeks

limes

red onion

red potatoes

shallots

sweet potatoes

tomatoes

turnips

yellow onions

the refrigerator & freezer

Once you have stocked and organized your pantry, you can apply the same time-saving principles to your refrigerator and freezer. Used for short-term cold storage, the refrigerator is ideal for keeping meats, poultry, dairy, vegetables, and leftovers fresh. The freezer will preserve most of the flavor and texture of meats, poultry, and many prepared dishes for 4 to 6 months if the foods are carefully packaged.

general tips

- Foods lose flavor under refrigeration, so proper storage and an even temperature of below 40°F (5°C) is important.

- Freeze foods at 0°F (-18°C) or below to retain color, texture, and flavor.

- Don't crowd foods in the refrigerator. Air must circulate freely to keep foods evenly cooled.

- To prevent freezer burn, use only moistureproof wrappings, such as aluminum foil, airtight plastic containers, or resealable plastic bags.

leftover storage

- You can store most prepared main dishes in an airtight container in the refrigerator for up to 4 days or in the freezer for up to 4 months.

- Check the contents of the refrigerator at least once a week and promptly discard old or spoiled food.

- Let food cool to room temperature before storing in the refrigerator or freezer. Transfer the cooled food to an airtight plastic or glass container, leaving room for expansion if freezing. Or, put the cooled food into a resealable plastic bag, expelling as much air as possible before sealing.

- Freeze some main dishes in small portions for when you need to heat up just enough to serve one or two people.

- Thaw frozen leftovers in the refrigerator or in the microwave. To avoid bacterial contamination, never thaw at room temperature.

FREEZING & THAWING

- For the best flavor and texture, freeze raw meat and poultry for no more than 6 months.

- Label all packages or containers with the date and contents before putting them in the freezer.

- Always thaw frozen meat and poultry in the refrigerator, never at room temperature or by placing them under warm or hot running water.

KEEP IT ORGANIZED

clean first Remove items and wash the refrigerator thoroughly with warm, soapy water, then rinse well with clear water. Wash and rinse your freezer at the same time.

rotate items Check the expiration dates on refrigerated items and discard any that have exceeded their time.

date of purchase Label items that you plan to keep for more than a week, writing the date directly on the package or on a piece of masking tape.

DAIRY

cheese: Cheddar, feta, goat, gruyére,

Monterey Jack, mozzarella, parmesan,

queso fresco, ricotta

eggs

heavy (double) cream

milk

sour cream

unsalted butter

FRUITS & VEGETABLES

bell peppers (capsicums)

broccoli

cabbage

carrots

cauliflower

celery

chiles, jalapeño or serrano

green (spring) onions

leeks

mushrooms

spinach

squashes

zucchini

FRESH HERBS

basil

cilantro (fresh coriander)

flat-leaf (Italian) parsley

thyme

CURED MEATS

pancetta or thick-cut bacon

prosciutto

fresh herb & vegetable storage

■ Trim the stem ends of a bunch of parsley, stand the bunch in a glass of water, drape a plastic bag loosely over the leaves, and refrigerate. Wrap other fresh herbs in a damp paper towel, slip into a plastic bag, and store in the crisper. Rinse and stem all herbs just before using.

■ Store tomatoes and eggplants (aubergines) at room temperature.

■ Cut about ½ inch (12 mm) off the end of each asparagus spear; stand the spears, tips up, in a glass of cold water; and refrigerate, changing the water daily. The asparagus will keep for up to 1 week.

■ Rinse leafy greens, such as chard, spin dry in a salad spinner, wrap in damp paper towels, and store in a resealable plastic bag in the crisper for up to 1 week. In general, store other vegetables in resealable bags in the crisper and rinse before using. Sturdy vegetables will keep for up to a week; more delicate ones will keep for only a few days.

cheese storage

■ Wrap all cheeses well to prevent them from drying out. Hard cheeses, such as Parmesan, have a low moisture content, so they keep longer than fresh cheeses, such as *queso fresco*. Use fresh cheeses within a couple of days. Store soft and semisoft cheeses, such as fontina, for up to 2 weeks and hard cheeses up to 1 month.

meat & poultry storage

■ Use fresh meat and poultry within 2 days of purchase. If using packaged meat, check the expiration date on the package and use before that date. Most seafood should be used the day of purchase.

■ To prevent cross-contamination with other foods, always place packaged meats on a plate in the coldest part of the refrigerator. Once you have opened the package, discard original wrappings and rewrap any unused portions in fresh wrapping.

index

Oxmoor
House ®

OXMOOR HOUSE

Oxmoor House books are distributed by Sunset Books
80 Willow Road, Menlo Park, CA 94025
Telephone: 650 321 3600 Fax: 650 324 1532

VP and Associate Publisher Jim Childs
Director of Sales Brad Moses
Oxmoor House and Sunset Books are divisions of
Southern Progress Corporation

WILLIAMS-SONOMA
Founder & Vice-Chairman Chuck Williams

THE WILLIAMS-SONOMA FOOD MADE FAST SERIES
Conceived and produced by Weldon Owen Inc.
814 Montgomery Street, San Francisco, CA 94133
Telephone: 415 291 0100 Fax: 415 291 8841

In collaboration with Williams-Sonoma, Inc.
3250 Van Ness Avenue, San Francisco, CA 94109

Photographers Tucker + Hossler
Food Stylist Jen Straus
Food Stylist's Assistant Alexa Hyman
Text Writer Kate Chynoweth

Library of Congress Cataloging-in-Publication data is available.
ISBN 13: 978-0-8487-3199-1
ISBN 10: 0-8487-3199-9

WELDON OWEN INC.

Chief Executive Officer John Owen
President and Chief Operating Officer Terry Newell
Chief Financial Officer Simon Fraser
Vice President Sales and New Business Development Amy Kaneko
Vice President and Creative Director Gaye Allen
Vice President and Publisher Hannah Rahill
Senior Editor Kim Goodfriend
Editor Lauren Hancock
Senior Designer and Photo Director Andrea Stephany
Designer Lauren Charles
Production Director Chris Hemesath
Color Manager Teri Bell
Production Manager Todd Rechner

A WELDON OWEN PRODUCTION
Copyright © 2008 by Weldon Owen Inc. and Williams-Sonoma, Inc.
All rights reserved, including the right of reproduction in
whole or in part in any form.

Set in Formata
First printed in 2008
10 9 8 7 6 5 4 3 2 1
Color separations by Bright Arts Singapore
Printed by Tien Wah Press

Printed in Singapore

ACKNOWLEDGMENTS
Weldon Owen wishes to thank the following people for their generous support in producing this book:
Heather Belt, Ken DellaPenta, Judith Dunham, Lesli Neilson, Sharon Silva, and Jason Wheeler.

A NOTE ON WEIGHTS AND MEASURES
All recipes include customary U.S. and metric measurements. Metric conversions are based on
a standard developed for these books and have been rounded off. Actual weights may vary.